100 Writing Mistakes to Avoid

(Revised Edition)

Maeve Maddox

DAEL Publications
Fayetteville, 2013

100 Writing Mistakes to Avoid
Revised Edition

ISBN: 1470137860
ISBN-13: 978-1470137861

FROM DIGITAL TO PRINT

100 Writing Mistakes to Avoid first appeared as an ebook published by Daniel Scocco, founder of the language blog DailyWritingTips.com/.

The new revised edition is available in both digital and print formats.

PART ONE

100 WRITING MISTAKES TO AVOID

PART TWO
BASIC ENGLISH GRAMMAR

PART ONE

100 WRITING MISTAKES TO AVOID

By
Maeve Maddox

•

INTRODUCTION

Not every writer needs to refer to a style guide as detailed as *The Chicago Manual of Style* (1,026 pages), or the *Associated Press Stylebook* (406 pages) on a daily basis. Those are for the hard questions. This guide, *100 Writing Mistakes to Avoid*, focuses on the most common errors that show up again and again in the media.

This list of spelling, usage, and punctuation mistakes does not include every possible error, but it covers a great many that can put off potential customers and clients.

A few of the entries discuss spelling or usage that differs in British and American English or represents usage on which thoughtful people disagree. These entries are marked with an asterisk (*). Writers may choose the form they prefer or, if they are writing for a client, follow a prescribed style guide.

Some recent idioms defy both English grammar and logic, but they are gaining wide acceptance. Entries relating to them are marked with a dagger (†). Careful speakers will continue to avoid them.

Word to the Wise: Parents, teachers, and employers are within their rights to correct nonstandard usage in the speech and writing of children, students, and staff who deal with the public, but it's bad manners to correct the usage of random adults.

Grammar terms and grammatical explanations have been kept to a minimum in *100 Mistakes*, but the reader is expected to be familiar with the English parts of speech and parts of the sentence. Simple explanations and examples of these basic concepts will be found in the bonus *Basic English Grammar* section of this book.

This little book cannot replace a dictionary or a premium stylebook, but the writer in a hurry can save time by looking here first.

Symbols

* thoughtful opinion differs as to acceptability

† widespread, but still not standard

1. SPELLING MISTAKES

a lot / alot

INCORRECT: I like you ~~alot~~.
CORRECT: I like you **a lot**.

Despite being used widely, "alot" is an incorrect spelling of *a lot.*

accept / except

INCORRECT: Please ~~except~~ this gift.
CORRECT: Please **accept** this gift.

Except, as a verb, means "to exclude" or "leave out." As a preposition it means "with the exception of."

Accept means "to receive willingly."

Examples of correct usage:
*We visited every landmark **except** the Eiffel Tower.*
*The school is **accepting** only those students who have had their shots; all others are **excepted**.*

advice / advise

INCORRECT: He refused to take my ~~advise~~.
CORRECT: He refused to take my **advice**.

Advise is a verb. The **s** has the sound of "z." *Advice* is a noun. The *c* has the sound of "s."

affect / effect

INCORRECT: His death really ~~effected~~ me.
CORRECT: His death really **affected** me.

The most common use of *effect* is as a noun meaning "something produced by a cause."

The most common use of *affect* is as a transitive verb meaning "to act upon."

Examples of correct usage:
*The disease had a lasting **effect** on the child. (noun)*
*You plans won't **affect** my actions.* (verb)

all right / alright

INCORRECT: He's ~~alright~~ after his fall.
CORRECT: He's **all right** after his fall.

Although arguments are advanced for the acceptance of the spelling, and it is often seen in television captions, "alright" is still widely regarded as nonstandard. Careful writers avoid it.

allude / elude / illude

INCORRECT: The writer ~~eluded~~ to the Odyssey.
CORRECT: The writer **alluded** to the Odyssey.

Elude means "to escape," usually by means of swift

or clever action. *Allude* means "to refer to indirectly." *Illude* is an obsolete spelling for *delude* and *elude*.

*** amok / amuck**

The more usual spelling is *amok*, but *amuck* is very common. Both are considered acceptable forms of this word borrowed from Malay.

awhile / a while

INCORRECT: I'll be staying in Paris ~~for awhile~~.

CORRECT: I'll be staying in Paris **for a while**.

CORRECT: Sit down and stay **awhile**.

Awhile is an adverb meaning "for a short time." *While* by itself is a noun meaning "a period of time."

cannot / can not

INCORRECT: I ~~can not~~ go with you today.

CORRECT: I **cannot** go with you today.

In speech and informal writing, *cannot* is frequently contracted as *can't*. In writing the uncontracted form, *cannot* is the preferred modern spelling.

complement / compliment

INCORRECT: I want to ~~complement~~ you on

your writing style.
CORRECT: I want to **compliment** you on your writing style.

Complement, most frequently used as a verb, means to complete or to add something needed.

Compliment, used as a verb, means "to make a courteous remark." As a noun, it means "a courteous remark."

Examples of correct usage:
*The illustrations **complement** the text.*
*She **complimented** his singing.*
*Sallie has difficulty accepting a **compliment**.*

definite / definate

INCORRECT: He won't give me a ~~definate~~ answer.
CORRECT: He won't give me a **definite** answer.

Spelling **definite** will be easier if one remembers that it is related to the words *finite* and *infinite*.

Something that is **infinite** has no limits. Something that is **finite** has limits. To define is to limit. Something that is definite is limited. Note the letter **i** in all these words.

every day / everyday

INCORRECT: Dan walks the dog ~~everyday~~ at

six p.m.

CORRECT: Dan walks the dog **every day** at six p.m.

Everyday is an adjective that means "daily."

Every day is a phrase that combines the adjective *every* with the noun *day*.

Examples of correct usage:
*Walking the dog is an **everyday** occurrence.*
*I practice the flute **every day**.*

forty/fourty

INCORRECT: She made the check out for ~~fourty~~ dollars.

CORRECT: She made the check out for **forty** dollars.

The numeral 4 is spelled *four*. The numeral 40 is spelled *forty*.

*** inquire / enquire**
These are two spellings of the same word.

Enquire tends to be more common in British usage, while *inquire* is more common in American usage.

The British newspaper *The Guardian* prefers *inquire*, and the *Oxford English Dictionary* considers *enquire* to be "an alternative form of *inquire*."

The forms *inquire* and *inquiry* are the safe choices when no official writing guidelines are being followed.

†irregardless / regardless

INCORRECT: I want you here at six a.m., ~~irregardless~~ of how late you go to bed tonight.
CORRECT: I want you here at six a.m., **regardless** of how late you go to bed tonight.

Although listed in dictionaries and widely used colloquially, the word "irregardless" is to be avoided as nonstandard usage. The prefix *-ir* and the suffix *-less* cancel each other out. Both are negatives. Saying "irregardless" is rather like saying "regardlessless."

its / it's

INCORRECT: Put the saw back in ~~it's~~ place.
CORRECT: put the saw back in **its** place.

It's is a contraction that represents two words: *it is*. *Its* is a one-word third-person singular possessive adjective, like *his*.

Examples of correct usage:
The dog wagged its tail.
It's too late to apologize.

NOTE: Of all the errors a writer or an advertiser

can make, the misuse of **it's** is probably the one most damaging to a person's professional credibility. Avoid it by never using a contraction for "it is." Always write out both words and, when proofing your work, always read **it's** aloud as "it is." That way you'll never put an apostrophe in the possessive adjective **its**.

*** judgment / judgement**

Both spellings are acceptable. British usage favors *judgement*; American usage favors *judgment.*

***license / licence**

> *license*: verb, "to grant permission"
> *licence*: noun, "permission, liberty"

In British usage, *licence* is the spelling of the noun and *license* is the spelling of the verb.

In American usage, both the noun and verb are spelled *license*.

lightning / lightening

> INCORRECT: The hen house was struck by ~~lightening~~ last night.
> CORRECT: The hen house was struck by **lightning** last night.

Lightening means "state of becoming brighter." *Lightning* means the flashing caused by an electrical discharge in the atmosphere.

Examples of correct use:
Thank you for **lightening** my load.
This dark room needs **lightening**.
His house has a **lightning** rod.

loose / lose

INCORRECT: Don't ~~loose~~ your way in the dark.

CORRECT: Don't **lose** your way in the dark.

As an adjective, *loose* means "not tight." The *s* is unvoiced (sounds like the *s* in *bus)*.

Lose is a verb. The *s* is voiced (sounds like the *s* in *his*). Meanings include "go astray from," "fail to keep up with," "suffer deprivation."

Examples of correct usage:
Athletes prefer ***loose*** *clothing for exercise.*
He frequently ***loses*** *his car keys.*

"ough" words

The words *thought, through, though, tough, rough,* and *cough* are often singled out as proof that English spelling is outrageously unphonetic.

The variety of sounds represented by the spelling *ough* in these words is undeniably strange, but the words are in such common use that the spellings have clung through several centuries. Banks and restaurants boast of "drive-thru" service, but in formal writing the spelling "thru" just doesn't look like a proper English word. If you are writing for a general audience, bite the bullet and go with the traditional **-ough** spellings.

passed / past

INCORRECT: The car ~~past~~ the train.
CORRECT: The car **passed** the train.

Past can be used as an adverb of place or as a preposition.

Passed is the past tense of the verb *to pass.* Because both words are pronounced the same, many writers have difficulty telling them apart without an understanding of the parts of speech. To use these words correctly, one must master the parts of speech.

Examples of correct usage:
*The **past** year has been hectic.* (adjective)
*The deadline has **passed**.* (past participle verb form)
*He **passed** her the biscuits.* (simple past verb form)
*The boys ran **past** the gate.* (preposition)
*As we stood in the doorway, the cat ran **past**.* (adverb)

pore / pour

INCORRECT: The students were up until midnight, ~~pouring~~ over their books.
CORRECT: The students were up until

midnight, **poring** over their books.

Pore is a verb meaning "to look at attentively." *Pour* is a verb meaning "to cause to flow."

prescibe / proscribe

INCORRECT: What did the doctor ~~proscribe~~ for your headache?

CORRECT: What did the doctor **prescribe** for your headache?

Prescribe in this context means "to give directions for." *Proscribe* means "to condemn or forbid as harmful." *The new statute proscribes employment discrimination.*

principle / principal

INCORRECT: The ~~principle~~ kept us after school.

CORRECT: The **principal** kept us after school.

As a noun, *principle* means "a general truth." As a noun referring to a person, *principal* is "the person in authority." The cloying but useful mnemonic for this one is *The princi**pal** is your pal.*

pronunciation / pronounciation

INCORRECT: I have trouble understanding his ~~pronounciation~~.

CORRECT: I have trouble understanding his **pronunciation**.

Although the verb is *pronounce*, the noun is

pronunciation.

quiet / quite

INCORRECT: We spent a ~~quite~~ evening reading.
CORRECT: We spent a **quiet** evening reading.

Quiet is an adjective meaning "marked by little or no activity." *Quite* is an adverb meaning "to a considerable extent." *Quiet* can also be used as a noun.

Examples of correct usage:
Jere was always a ***quiet*** *child. (*adjective*)*
Can't you ***quiet*** *those dogs? (*verb*)*
We enjoyed the ***quiet*** *by the lake.* (noun)

separate / seperate

INCORRECT: The troupe members demanded ~~seperate~~ accommodations.
CORRECT: The troupe members demanded **separate** accommodations.

A useful mnemonic:
There's **a rat** in sep-**a-rat**e.

than / then

INCORRECT: I have more eggs ~~then~~ you.
CORRECT: I have more eggs **than** you.

Than in a comparison is a connecting word that

introduces the second part of a comparison. *Then* is an adverb of time. *Than* is followed by a noun or a pronoun, which may be an object or the subject of an unexpressed verb.

Examples of correct usage:
Charlie is a better player ***than*** *he [is].*
She likes me better than him.
She likes cats better ***than*** *dogs.*

The man paused by the door, and ***then*** *entered.* (adverb of time followed by the verb it modifies)
So, what did you do ***then****?* (adverb of time modifying the verb that precedes it)

there / they're / their

INCORRECT: They parked ~~there~~ car on the lawn.

CORRECT: They parked **their** car on the lawn.

There is an adverb of place. It can stand anywhere in a sentence. *They're* is a contraction of "they are." *Their* is a possessive adjective. It must be followed by a noun.

Examples of correct usage:
I *don't know why* ***they're*** *always late.* (contraction)
Tell them to put ***their*** *coats on the bed.* (possessive adjective)
I don't want to go ***there****.* (adverb of place)

to / two / too

INCORRECT: I'm ~~to~~ tired to go out again.
CORRECT: I'm **too** tired to go out again.

To is a preposition that indicates direction. It is also a particle used with a verb infinitive. *Too* is an adverb used to indicate excess. *Two* is the spelling of the numeral 2.

Examples of correct usage:
Let's all go ***to*** *the lobby. (preposition)*
Remember ***to brush*** *your teeth. (infinitive use)*
They ate ***too*** *much pizza. (adverb)*
You may have ***two*** *pieces. (numerical adjective)*

weather / whether / wether

INCORRECT: He never knows ~~weather~~ to phone or just drop by.
CORRECT: He never knows **whether** to phone or just drop by.

Weather is a noun that refers to the state of the atmosphere. It may also be used, literally or figuratively, as a verb with the meaning "to stand up to and survive."
Whether is a function word with various uses.
Wether is a castrated sheep or goat.

Examples of correct usage:
When will you know ***whether*** *you can come?*
The ***weather*** *should be mild this weekend.*

The passengers ***weathered*** *the storm without too much sickness.*
The ***belwether*** *led the flock.*

Wednesday / Wenesday

INCORRECT: The concert has been moved to ~~Wenesday~~.
CORRECT: The concert has been moved to **Wednesday**.

Some native English speakers pronounce the *d* in *Wednesday*, but many others do not.Whether you say Wed-nes-day or Wens-day, spell it *Wed-nes-day*. The ***d*** is there because the word was originally "Woden's day."

who's / whose

INCORRECT: I don't know ~~who's~~ dog you're talking about.
CORRECT: I don't know **whose** dog you're talking about.

Who's is the contracted form of *who is*.
Whose is the possessive adjective form of *who*.

Examples of correct usage:
Who's *your daddy?* (contraction)
Whose *car are we going in?* (adjective)

wreck / wreak

INCORRECT: The wizard plans to ~~wreck~~

vengeance on the outlanders.
CORRECT: The wizard plans to **wreak** vengeance on the outlanders.

Wreck, as a verb, means "to reduce to a ruinous state by violence." It is pronounced with a short e, rhyming with *neck*.

Wreak means "to inflict" or "bring about." It is pronounced with a long e, rhyming with *sneak*.

writing/writting

INCORRECT: How are you coming with your ~~writting~~?
CORRECT: How are you coming with your **writing**?

In the word *write*, the **e** at the end indicates that the preceding vowel is long. (Long vowel sounds correspond to the name of the letter when it is recited in the alphabet: A, E, I, O, U.)

Dropping the **e** of **write** and adding **-ing** retains the long **i** sound. Doubling the **t** changes the long **i** of **write** into the short sound of **writ** (rhymes with "nit.") The **t** is correctly doubled when forming the past participle form **written**.

your / you're

INCORRECT: Give me ~~you're~~ advice.
CORRECT: Give me **your** advice.

You're is a contraction that represents the words *you are*.
Your is the second person plural possessive adjective.

Examples of correct usage:
You're *my best friend.* (contraction)
Is that **your** *key on the ground?* (possessive adjective)

2. USAGE MISTAKES

a / an

INCORRECT: Meet me here in ~~a~~ hour.
CORRECT: Meet me here in **an** hour.

The rule is to use the article **a** before words that begin with a consonant sound, and **an** before words beginning with a vowel sound:
***a** dog*
***an** eel*
***an** hour*

NOTE: A vowel sound is produced without any friction from the speech organs. A consonant sound is formed by contact or friction with the tongue, lips, or other speech organs.

Only a few English words begin with an unvoiced ("silent") **h**:
***an** heir to the throne*
***an** honest man*
***an** honorable man.*

The same principles of pronunciation apply to abbreviations, acronyms and the like:
a *URL (although U is a vowel letter, it is pronounced with the consonant sound of Y)*
an *@ symbol (the symbol represents the word "at," which begins with a vowel sound)*
an *SUV (S is a consonant letter, but its pronunciation begins with a vowel sound: ess).*

abstract nouns ending with -ness

INCORRECT: Anwar Sadat was admired for his ~~courageousness~~.

CORRECT: Anwar Sadat was admired for his **courage**.

The suffix **-ness** is correctly added to many adjectives to form a corresponding abstract noun.

For example,
good/goodness,
red/redness.

However, many English adjectives already have a corresponding abstract noun form that does not end in **-ness**. Writers will develop a stronger style by learning the abstract forms that already exist.

Examples of adjective/abstract noun pairs:
silent/silence
curious/curiosity
brave/bravery
courageous/courage

valiant, valor
cowardly, cowardice
greedy/greed
mature/maturity.

A few abstract nouns are the same as the corresponding adjective. For example,
We enjoyed the ***calm*** *atmosphere at the cove.* (adjective)
The cove was a place of peace and ***calm****.* (noun)
The ***cool*** *breeze was welcome after the hot day.* (adjective)
We enjoyed walking there in the ***cool*** *of the evening.* (noun)

†anyway/anyways/any way

INCORRECT: Who reads my paper ~~anyways~~?
CORRECT:Who reads my paper **anyway**?

Anyway is an adverb meaning "regardless" or "in any event":

Any way is a phrase meaning "any particular course, direction, or manner." Examples of correct usage:
Our dog tries to get out of his pen ***any way*** *he can.* (phrase)
*Penelope never completes her homework assignments, but she expects to go to college anyway. (*adverb*)*

"Anyways" is a nonstandard form of the adverb

anyway.

averse / adverse

INCORRECT: I'm not ~~adverse~~ to a glass of wine at dinner
CORRECT: I'm not **averse** to a glass of wine at dinner.

Averse is an adjective meaning "having an active feeling of repugnance or dislike."

Adverse is an adjective meaning "being in opposition to one's interests."

Examples of correct usage:
*Is he **averse** to eating meat?* ("opposed to")
*Do you think the judge will deliver an **adverse** opinion?* ("unfavorable")

†beg the question / raise the question
To beg the question is a rhetorical term to describe the logical fallacy of assuming the truth of an unsupported assertion. For example,
Professor Jones grades unfairly because he never gives me any grade higher than a C on my papers.

The unproved assumption is that the papers are of a quality to merit a higher grade. The student is "begging the question."

In ordinary conversation, many speakers now use

the expression "to beg the question" as if it meant "to ask the question" or "to raise the question." For example,

His position on tax reform begs the question, does wealth redistribution really help the poor?

Incorrect or not, this use of *to beg the question* is now in wide use on both sides of the Atlantic. The shift from its original rhetorical meaning may derive from association with the expression "I beg your pardon."

It seems to me that this is one of those errors that people who know better may choose to avoid, but which has reached a tipping point in common speech that makes continued criticism of it futile.

between you and me / I

INCORRECT: Keep this information just ~~between you and I.~~
CORRECT: Keep this information just **between you and me.**

Between is a preposition. *Me* is the object form of the pronoun *I.* When a pronoun follows a preposition, the object form is required.

bring / take

INCORRECT: We're going to ~~bring~~ ice cream to the party.

CORRECT: We're going to **take** ice cream to the party.

The choice between *bring* and *take* depends upon the location of the speaker. If the action is moving from the speaker to another location, then the word *take* is called for.

If the action is coming towards the speaker, the choice is *bring*.

Examples of correct usage:
Bring *me the book when you come to my house tonight.*
Take *the book with you when you leave.*

***can/may**

He wants to know if he can borrow the car tonight.
He wants to know if he may borrow the car tonight.

The difference between *can* and *may* is one of ability versus permission. Not all native speakers observe the distinction, but it is a graceful usage.

***could care less / couldn't care less**
Much breath and ink are expended in arguing about this expression, yet both forms have been in the language for more than half a century, and both are used with exactly the same meaning.

Pedants argue that "I could care less" is illogical because if one could care less, one therefore cares a little.

When it comes to idiom, logic is frequently irrelevant. Whether the "not" appears or not, speakers who use the expression are not chopping logic. What they mean is that they don't care.

Linguist Mark Liberman estimates that in American English, the use of "could care less" exceeds that of "couldn't care less" by a ratio of about 5 to 1.

Speakers who prefer "could care less" to "couldn't care less" shuld not be intimidated by the "couldn't care less" faction; either version is acceptable in standard English. Students, however, are advised to avoid the expression, as many English teachers feel strongly about the subject.

*** different from / different to / different than**
Preferred by H. W. Fowler in his landmark *Modern English Usage,* the form *different from* is considered by many speakers, both British and American, to be the only correct form of the comparative phrase. However, *different to* is quite common among British speakers and *different than* among American.

According to *AskOxford*, "There is little difference

in sense between *different from*, *different to*, and *different than*. *Different from* is generally regarded as the correct use in British English, while *different than* is largely restricted to North America."

†disinterested / uninterested

INCORRECT: Charlie is totally ~~disinterested~~ in algebra.
CORRECT: Charlie is totally **uninterested** in algebra.

Disinterested implies impartiality. *Uninterested* implies lack of interest.
Examples of correct usage:
The financial dispute was settled by a ***disinterested*** *third party.*

Many students are ***uninterested*** *in their assignments.*

Careful writers and speakers continue to observe this useful distinction.

double negative

INCORRECT: I ~~don't get no~~ respect.
CORRECT: I **don't get any** respect.

Although common in regional dialects and in earlier forms of English, the use of a double negative is considered to be incorrect in modern standard English.

economic / economical

INCORRECT: Eating at home is more ~~economic~~ than dining out.
CORRECT: Eating at home is more **economical** than dining out.

Economic refers to economics and the economy. *Economical* refers to getting the most value for one's money.

e.g. / i.e.

INCORRECT: Boswell asked Dr. Johnson about every trivial detail, *(~~e.g.,~~* he made himself a daily nuisance).
CORRECT: Boswell asked Dr. Johnson about every trivial detail, (***i.e.***, he made himself a daily nuisance).

The abbreviation *e.g.* stands for the Latin expression *exempli gratia* and means "for example." The abbreviation *i.e.* stands for the Latin expression *id est* ("it is") and is used in English to mean "in other words."

either is / either are

INCORRECT: Either Jack or Joan ~~are~~ correct.
CORRECT: Either Jack or Joan **is** correct.

Either, which may be either a pronoun or an adjective, is singular. Its meaning is "each of the two."

When *either* introduces a choice between two things, the verb must be singular:
Either *the Honda or the Ford* ***belongs*** *to Harry.*
Either *one of the books* ***is*** *a good choice.*

Confusion arises when *either* introduces an *either...or* construction in which one of the choices is singular and one is plural. In such a case, the verb will agree with the nearer noun:
Either hot dogs or pizza ***is*** *on the menu for tonight.*
Either pizza or hot dogs ***are*** *on the menu for tonight.*

Neither, like *either*, is a singular word that usually takes a singular verb. In a *neither...nor* construction that contains a singular noun and a plural noun, the verb agrees with the nearer noun:

Neither bad morals nor ***hypocrisy is*** *wanted in a public official.*
Neither hypocrisy nor ***bad morals are*** *wanted in a public official.*

*** farther/further**
Farther and *further* can be used interchangeably as adverbs meaning "at a more advanced point":
He rode farther down the road.
He rode further down the road.

They can also be used as adjectives:
Little Rock is farther south than Russellville.

Oklahoma is further west than Tennessee.

When the context is figurative or abstract, *further* is preferred:
This restaurant will be closed until further notice.
This broken rake is of no further use to me.

As a verb, *further* means "to help forward, to assist." For example,
He would stop at nothing to further his ambition.

flammable / inflammable

INCORRECT: These pajamas ~~can't burn~~ because they're ~~inflammable~~.
CORRECT: These pajamas **can burn** because they're **inflammable**.

Both words, *flammable* and *inflammable*, mean "capable of bursting into flames." In modern usage the term *inflammable* is being dropped because its prefix ***-in,*** which here means "into" is often confused with the prefix *-in* that means "not."

To avoid dangerous misunderstanding in advertising, the better practice is to use *nonflammable* as the opposite of *flammable*.

† free rein / free reign

INCORRECT: Unfortunately, their parents give them ~~free reign~~ on the weekends.
CORRECT: Unfortunately, their parents give

them **free rein** on the weekends.

Free rein is a term that originated with horse riding. It refers to holding the horse's reins loosely, so as to permit the horse to move more freely. The figurative sense relates to any kind of unimpeded freedom.
Reign refers to the authority of a monarch.

NOTE: The incorrect "free reign" is becoming so common that it will probably reach a tipping point of acceptability. Writers who understand the difference will observe it, but it's probably futile to rail against writers who don't.

good / better / best

INCORRECT: Who's the ~~best~~ runner, Jack or Jill?
CORRECT: Who's the **better** runner, Jack or Jill?

Good has the irregular comparative forms *better* and *best.*

Better is used to compare two people or things: *This rope is better than that one.*

Best is used to compare three or more people or things: *Charlie is the best player on the football team.*

good / well

INCORRECT: I hope I did ~~good~~ on the exam.

CORRECT: I hope did **well** on the exam.

Good is an adjective.
Well is an adverb.

Examples of correct usage:
That chicken tastes good. (adjective describing a noun)
You drive very well. (adverb describing an action)

historic / historical

INCORRECT: The signing of the bill today is a ~~historical~~ event.

CORRECT: The signing of the bill today is a **historic** event.

Historical is an adjective that refers to anything that has happened in the past.

Historic is an adjective that describes an event or invention that had or will have a major impact on human life.

Examples of correct usage:
The novel is based on historical events in the settling of the American West.
The driving of the Golden Spike was a historic event.
NOTE: Some speakers use the article *an* before the words *historic* and *historical*. This usage is old-

fashioned, but acceptable.

*** hopefully / thankfully**
These words are often criticized when used to comment on a sentence. For example,
Hopefully I'll be able to join you at seven.
Thankfully, no one was hurt.

The objection brought is that *hopefully* should mean only "full of hope" and *thankfully* "full of thanks." In fact the words conform to the same condensed expression as *frankly* and *luckily*, shortened forms of "to speak frankly," and "as luck would have it."

incident / incidence

> INCORRECT: The witness described the ~~incidence~~ to the police.
> CORRECT: The witness described the **incident** to the police.

Incidence is a noun meaning "the extent of something's influence."

Incident is a noun meaning "an occurrence or an event."

Examples of correct usage:
The incident involved a trailer truck and a Miata.
What is the incidence of poverty among women?

imply / infer

INCORRECT: His use of that word ~~infers~~ that he doesn't trust you.
CORRECT: His use of that word **implies** that he doesn't trust you.

Imply means to suggest a meaning. The person who *implies* something hints at it without saying it directly.

Infer means to take meaning from. The person who *infers* draws a conclusion by interpreting words or actions.

Examples of correct usage:
Because you are always late, I infer that you don't want to work here.
His tone of voice seemed to imply that I'd done something wrong.

in / on

INCORRECT: The ship is sailing ~~in~~ the water.
CORRECT: The ship is sailing **on** the water.
The use of prepositions in English is frequently idiomatic. General guidelines exist, but they cannot cover all the expressions involving prepositions.

In usually denotes "state of being somewhere within."
On usually indicates "proximity and position,

above or outside."

lend / loan / borrow

INCORRECT: Will you ~~**borrow**~~ me your pen for a minute?
CORRECT: Will you **lend** me your pen for a minute?

Lend means "to grant the temporary possession of a thing. *Borrow* means "to take a thing with the intention of returning it."

As a noun, *loan* is what is borrowed. *Loan* in the sense of "lend" is U.S. usage. Some authorities do not accept *loan* as a verb.

† **less / fewer**

INCORRECT: This box contains ~~less~~ fire crackers.
CORRECT: This box contains **fewer** fire crackers.

Less is used with uncounted nouns:
less soup
less intelligence
less forage

Fewer is used with countable nouns:
fewer voters
fewer apples
fewer commercials

The misuse of *less* and *few* is extremely widespread, but many speakers feel strongly about observing the traditional rule. Advertisers who don't want to alienate consumers would do well to learn the difference.

***mankind/humankind**

Mankind has been used for many generations with the meaning of "all humankind." In recent years, however, many English speakers have come to feel that *mankind* excludes women.

Modern usage seems to prefer *humankind* as a more gender-neutral choice.

Miss / Mrs / Ms

> INCORRECT: Address the letter to ~~Miss~~ Jones.
> CORRECT: Address the letter to **Ms**. Jones.

Miss, denoting an unmarried woman, is an honorific no longer considered acceptable in common use because it identifies a woman according to marital status.
Mrs., denoting a married woman, is considered unacceptable for the same reason.
Ms. is an honorific like *Mr*. that indicates gender without revealing marital status.

NOTE: In American usage, Ms. and Mrs. are written with periods. In British usage the periods are omitted.

people / persons

INCORRECT: I don't know any of the ~~persons~~ in this room.

CORRECT: I don't know any of the **people** in this room.

Although the plural of *person* is *persons*, in most non-legal contexts *people* is the preferred plural of *person*.

Scotch / Scots / Scottish

INCORRECT: The ~~Scotch~~ people value education.

CORRECT: The **Scottish** people value education.

CORRECT: The **Scots** value education.

Scotch is an adjective still used in certain established expressions such as *Scotch whisky* and *Scotch broth*.

In other contexts it is considered undesirable to speak of "Scotchmen" or "the Scotch government." Use *Scots* or *Scottish* in a general context to convey the idea of belonging to or being from Scotland:
a Scotswoman
The Scotsman (newspaper)
the Scottish weather
the Scottish parliament

The word for the nationality is *Scots*.

sooner than / when

INCORRECT: No sooner had the dog catcher turned his back, ~~when~~ the boy released the stray.

CORRECT: No sooner had the dog catcher turned his back, **than** the boy released the stray.

Modern usage prefers *than* to *when* as the conjunction to be used in this expression.

***their with singular antecedent**

Writers of English have been using "their" with singular antecedents for centuries. For example,

> *Every one* in the House *were* in *their* beds. --Henry Fielding, *Tom Jones* (1749)

> *A person* can't help *their* birth. --William Thackeray, *Vanity Fair* (1847)

> It's enough to drive *anyone* out of *their* senses. --George Bernard Shaw, *Candida* (1898)

> She kept her head and kicked her shoes off, as *everybody* ought to do who falls into deep water in *their* clothes. --C.S. Lewis, *The Voyage of the Dawn Treader* (1952)

Ungrammatical or not, this use of **their** is idiomatic. Writers who are bothered by the lack of agreement are free to reorder their sentences in order to avoid it.

A sentence such as, ***Every voter*** *should exercise* ***their*** *right to vote* is easily rewritten by putting it in the plural: ***All voters*** *should exercise* ***their*** *right to vote.*

† there is / are

> INCORRECT: ~~There's~~ some children at the door.
> CORRECT: **There are** some children at the door.

When the word *there* is used to begin a sentence, the verb that follows should agree with the true subject of the sentence.
NOTE: *There* is often used as a sentence opener, but the true subject of the sentence comes later in the sentence:

There is a cat on the fence. ("cat" is the true subject)
There are six cookies left. ("cookies" is the true subject)

In spoken English it is easy to begin "there" sentences with the contraction "there's," regardless of whether the subject word is singular or plural.

In writing, there's no reason not to make the "to be" verb agree in number with the true subject of the sentence. Stylistically speaking, sentences that begin with "there" do not represent strong writing and are better rewritten to put the true subject at the beginning.

these / those

These is the plural of *this*. Used as either a demonstrative adjective or a demonstrative pronoun, *these* indicates objects or persons near to the speaker.

Those is the plural of *that*. Used as either a demonstrative adjective or a demonstrative pronoun, *those* indicates objects or persons away from the speaker.

Used together, *these* and *those* indicate contrast or opposition: *Do you want these or those?*

waiting on / waiting for

> INCORRECT: We ~~waited on the bus~~, but it never came.
> CORRECT: We **waited for the bus**, but it never came.

W*ait on* means "to serve."
The woman waited on the customer.

Wait for implies expectation or anticipation. *The child is waiting for Santa Claus.*

3. GRAMMAR MISTAKES

dangling participle

INCORRECT: *Reported missing a month ago, police have recovered the body of a young girl.*
CORRECT: *The body of a young girl reported missing a month ago has been recovered by police.*
CORRECT: *Police have recovered the body of a young girl reported missing a month ago.*

Verb forms ending in *-ing* or *-ed* are called participles. They can be used as adjectives, either alone or as the first word in a descriptive phrase. A common error is to follow a participial phrase with the wrong noun. The sense here is that the "girl" (not the "police") has been reported missing.

† if I was / if I were

INCORRECT: ~~If I was~~ a rich man, I'd buy houses for all my children.
CORRECT: **If I were** a rich man, I'd buy

houses for all my children.

Although more and more English speakers fail to observe the use of *were* in an **if clause** that makes a statement contrary to fact, it's a usage that careful writers will probably continue to observe.

If the statement is contrary to fact, use *were*.

In some contexts the **if clause** may contain a factual statement for which "was" is the suitable choice, for example,

If I was listening at the door, I had my reasons.

(The speaker was in fact listening at the door.)

† if I would / if I had/if I did

INCORRECT: I~~f I would have known~~ about the party, I would have gone to it.

CORRECT: **If I had known** about the party, I would have gone to it.

When speaking of an event that might have happened in the past but didn't, we use an **if clause** containing the helping verb "had" followed by a main clause containing "would":

If I had known you were coming, I would have baked a cake.

This use is sometimes called the "third conditional."

Another error made with the third conditional is to use the auxiliary "did" in the if clause:

INCORRECT: ~~If Captain Jones **didn't pull me**~~ from that burning car, I would be dead.
CORRECT: If Captain Jones **hadn't pulled me** from that burning car, I would be dead.

† **lay / lie** (to recline)

INCORRECT: I think I'll ~~lay down~~ for a few minutes.
CORRECT: I think I'll **lie down** for a few minutes.

Lay is the past tense of the verb *to lie*, "to recline."
Examples of correct usage of the forms of *to lie* (to recline):
*Today I lie in the hammock. (*present declarative*)*
*I am lying happily in the sun. (*present continuous*)*
*Lie down, Fido! (*present imperative)
*Yesterday I lay in the hammock. (*simple past*)*
*I have lain in the hammock for hours. (*present perfect*)*
I had lain in the hammock only a few moments when the phone rang. (past perfect)

† **lay/lie** ("to place")

INCORRECT: ~~Lie~~ the book on the table.
CORRECT: **Lay** the book on the table.

Lay is the present tense of the verb *to lay,* "to place."
Examples of correct usage of the forms of *to lay* (to place)
Watch me lay the book on the table.
Yesterday I laid the book on the table.

I have already laid the book on the table.
I am laying the book on the table.

NOTE: The misuse of *lay* (transitive verb) and *lie* (intransitive verb) is widespread in the popular media, but advertisers and writers know that errors with these verbs still pr ovoke criticism from consumers and readers. Conscientious writers will take the trouble to learn the difference.

me / I

INCORRECT: ~~Me and Jamie are going~~ to Mexico.
CORRECT: **Jamie and I are going** to Mexico.

Me and *I* are two forms of the same pronoun: the pronoun that stands for the person speaking. Which one to use depends upon the word's function.

Correct uses of **me**:
*Did you see **me** at the ball game yesterday?* (direct object of the verb "see")
*Please give **me** an answer soon.* (indirect object of the verb give)
*That's not a very good picture of **me**.* (object of the preposition "of")

Correct uses of **I**:
***I** am going to Mexico.* (subject of the verb "am going")

*Jamie and **I** are going to Mexico.* (subject, with "Jamie," of the verb "are going")

Few native speakers above the age of three would say, *Me rode the trolley,* but many adults will say, *Me and Jamie rode the trolley.*

This incorrect use of *me* may be deliberate with some speakers who wish to emulate uneducated celebrities.

For other speakers, the problem may be simply not knowing how to deal with a compound subject.

One way to avoid using *me* as a subject when speaking of oneself and someone else is to put the other person first. By beginning the sentence with the other person's name, the speaker has a better likelihood of choosing the correct form of the pronoun because it will come closer to the verb:
Jamie and I rode the trolley.
Jamie and I are going to Mexico.

*** Microsoft is / are**

> AMERICAN USAGE: *Microsoft is settling with another software distributor.*
> BRITISH USAGE: *Microsoft are settling with another software distributor.*

In British English, collective nouns and the names of organizations can take either a singular or plural verb, depending upon whether the entity is being thought of as a single thing or as a collection of individual things or persons.

In American usage, such words almost always take a singular verb.

myself / I

INCORRECT: ~~Sophie and myself volunteer~~ three days a month at the homeless shelter.
CORRECT: **Sophie and I volunteer** three days a month at the homeless shelter.

Myself is a pronoun whose function is to restate the subject of the sentence:

I cut myself shaving.
Sometimes I talk to myself as I work.
I wouldn't have believed it myself.
Before using **myself**, be sure that **I** has already been mentioned.

*** none is / none are**

Strictly speaking, *none* is singular. Its literal meaning is "not one," but as used in English, *none* may also be understood as "not any."

When *none* is used to emphasize the individuals in a group, it will take a singular verb: *None of the scouts has remembered to bring his lanyard.* (singular)

When the intent is to emphasize a group, *none* takes a plural verb: *None of the board members agree on the tuition hike*. (plural)

Used with an uncountable noun, *none* takes a singular verb: *None of the soup is left*.

*** preposition at the end of a sentence**
Many writers go to great lengths in the effort to avoid ending a sentence with a preposition in the belief that to do so is to break a rule of "good English." This belief is misplaced. It arose from the practice of 17th century writers like John Dryden (1631-1700) whose familiarity with and admiration for Latin led them to attempt to apply rules of Latin grammar to the writing of English. The result was often at odds with English idiom. It's past time to stop wasting breath and ink on this old chestnut.

ran/run

INCORRECT: The dog ~~has ran~~ away.
CORRECT: The dog **has run** away.

Run is an irregular verb whose past participle form (run) is the same as the present form. The simple past is *ran*.

Examples of the correct use of the forms of *run*:
Today I run.
Yesterday I ran.

I have run every day this week.

A common error is to use the simple past (*ran*) when the past participle (*run*) is called for. The form *ran* should never be used with the helping verbs *has, have*, or *had*.

Other irregular verbs susceptible to the same kind of error with the past participle are *go, come, write, give*, *drink*, and *eat*. The correct use of these verbs with the helping verb *have* or *had* are:
have gone
have come
have written
have given
have drunk
have eaten.

should have / should of

INCORRECT: I ~~should of listened~~ to my instincts.
CORRECT: I **should have listened** to my instincts.

The contraction *should've* combines the words *should* and *have*.

superlatives

INCORRECT: This movie is the ~~most awesomest~~ I've ever seen.
CORRECT: This movie is the **most awesome**

I've ever seen.

Adjectives have three forms: *positive, comparative*, and *superlative*.

Positive, the adjective's "plain" form. For example, *awesome.*
Comparative, the form used to compare two things: For example, *more awesome.*
Superlative, the form used to compare more than two things: For example, *most awesome.*
Adjectives of one syllable (and some two-syllable adjectives) form their comparisons by adding the endings **-er** and **-est**:
This is a fine story.
This is a finer story than that one.
This is the finest story of all.
This is a simple solution.
This is a simpler solution.
This is the simplest solution of all.

Adjectives of two or more syllables form their comparisons with ***more*** or ***most***.
Joe's ladder is unsafe.
Sam's ladder is more unsafe than Joe's
Sally's ladder is the most unsafe of all.
This is a beautiful flower.
This is a more beautiful flower than that one.
This is the most beautiful flower of all.

More and more native English speakers seem to be

disregarding the conventional forms of comparison. Constructions like "a lot more colder" and "the most awesomest" are often seen on the web. They may be meant to be humorous, but they come across as babyish.

†supposed to / suppose to

INCORRECT: ~~I'm suppose to wash~~ the windows on Saturday.

CORRECT: **I'm supposed to wash** the windows on Saturday.

Suppose is a verb. Used with a helping verb, it takes the past participle ending: **-ed**. The participle form in **-ed** can be used as an adjective:

an old-fashioned girl
a well-seasoned steak

*** toward / towards**

Towards may be more common among British speakers, but, used prepositionally, both are acceptable.

The child ran towards the road.
The child ran toward the road.

went / gone

INCORRECT: Fame ~~had went~~ to his head.

CORRECT: Fame **had gone** to his head.

The verb *go* has irregular past and past participle forms. The simple past is *went*. The past participle form is (had) *gone*.

which / that

INCORRECT: That's the boy ~~which~~ started the fire.

CORRECT: That's the boy **who** started the fire.

That is a pronoun that can stand for either people or things

Which is used for inanimate things only.

Either *that* or *which* may be used to introduce a clause that contributes essential information to a sentence.

NOTE: There is a modern tendency to prefer *that* in such sentences, but *which* is also acceptable.

A clause that contributes essential information is called a **restrictive** or **essential clause**.

The first car that I looked at did not have seat belts.

The clause "that I looked at" is restrictive because it adds essential information to the subject word "car."

When the clause is **non-restrictive (non-essential)**, *which* is used to introduce it:

The dinner, which my uncle paid for, was outrageously expensive.

Notice that in this sentence the *which* clause is set off by commas. It contains information that may be left out without affecting the sense of the main clause. The clause is, therefore, a non-restrictive clause.

*** who / that**

CORRECT: The woman **who** sold you the car didn't own it.
ALSO CORRECT: The woman **that** sold you the car didn't own it.

I've seen impassioned blog posts and comments on the correctness or incorrectness of using *that* instead of *who* to stand for a person. *Who* is the usual pronoun for people, but sometimes there are stylistic reasons for choosing *that*.

†who / whom

INCORRECT: ~~Whom~~ shall I say is calling?
CORRECT: **Who** shall I say is calling?

Whom is the object form of the pronoun *who*. Like *me, him, her, us*, and *them*, its correct grammatical use is to serve as the object of a verb or a preposition.
***Whom** do you mean?* (direct object of the verb "do mean")
*To **whom** shall I give this puppy?* (object of the preposition "to")
*That is the man **whom** I saw running away*. (object of the verb "saw.")

Because so many speakers and writers of standard English have come to use *who* as both subject and object, it's no longer seen as an error to use *who* as the object of a verb. Unfortunately, some speakers and writers mistakenly try to use *whom* as a subject. For example, *Whom shall I say is calling?*

The sentence is made up of two clauses, each of which has a pronoun as its subject. The verbs are *shall say* and *is calling*.

The subject of *shall say* is correctly given as *I*.

The subject of *is calling*, however, cannot be *whom* because *whom* is an object form. The corrected sentence would read, *Who shall I say is calling?*

Perhaps the easiest way to avoid using *whom* incorrectly is not to use *whom* at all. Apart from some established expressions such as "to whom it may concern" or "for whom the bell tolls," the use of "who" as an object probably goes unnoticed by most listeners or readers.

4. PUNCTUATION MISTAKES

apostrophe to form plural

INCORRECT: King Alfred the Great lived in the ~~800's.~~

CORRECT: King Alfred the Great lived in the **800s**.

Current usage avoids the use of an apostrophe to form the plural of letters or numerals. The only time to use an apostrophe to form a plural is to form the plurals of lower-case letters. Compare:
I can't tell your is from your es.
I can't tell your i's from your e's.

apostrophe to form possessive

INCORRECT: Mr. Thomas' opinion was that the dog should be returned.

> CORRECT: Mr. Thomas's opinion was that the dog should be returned.

Singular nouns that do not end in **s** form the possessive by adding the apostrophe plus an **s ('s)**:
Mary's veil.
The house's roof.
The trunk's latch.

Plural nouns that end in **s** form the possessive by adding an apostrophe:
The birds' beaks.
The teachers' salaries.
The street lamps' bulbs.

A few nouns do not form the plural by adding s. Their possessive is formed by adding apostrophe **s ('s)**:
The children's teacher.
The deer's meadow.
The salesmen's catalogs.

Singular nouns that end in **s** form the possessive by adding apostrophe **s ('s)**:
St. James's Park.

NOTE: Not all authorities agree that the addition of *'s* to a singular noun ending in *s* should be a hard and fast rule.
The British *Penguin Guide to Punctuation* states this rule:

> *...a name ending in s takes only an apostrophe*

if the possessive form is not pronounced with an extra s.
Hence:
Socrates' philosophy
Ulysses' companions

The reasoning is that one doesn't say "Socrateses" or "Ulysseses," so the extra *s* should not be added.

Most style books directed at speakers of American English disregard pronunciation, ruling that any singular noun ending in s will form its possessive by adding *'s*.

Not all speakers of American English agree. For example, U.S. Supreme Court Justice Thomas insists on the form "Chief Justice Thomas' opinion."

The best advice is to choose your syle book and be consistent.

colon
The most common use of a colon is to introduce a list following an independent clause.
The winners are the following films: The Lion King, Silas Marner, and *Kim.*
The next most common use of the colon is to separate an example, explanation, or reason from a preceding independent clause:
It's over between us: you won't stop drinking to

excess.
I learned a useful mnemonic for remembering the colors of the rainbow: Roy G. Biv.

Some other uses of the colon:
• between the numbers in the time: *8:30 a.m.*
• after the salutation in a business letter: *Dear Mr. Patel:*
• in memo headings: *Re: TO: SUBJECT:*
• in Biblical references: *Hebrews 13:8*

Comma - Uses and Common Errors
comma splice

> INCORRECT: The fire truck tore around the corner, flames spurted from the burning car.
> CORRECT: The fire truck tore around the corner. Flames spurted from the burning car.

A comma splice occurs when two independent clauses are joined by a comma. There are various ways to correct a comma splice. The easiest is to change the comma to a period and capitalize the next word.

comma missing after introductory clause

> INCORRECT: If I were you I'd do what you have done.
> CORRECT: If I were you, I'd do what you have done.

An adverbial clause that begins a sentence is set off by a comma: *When the rains came, everyone stayed inside.*

comma missing after introductory words/phrases/clauses

INCORRECT: If you want to pass the exam you will have to study harder.

CORRECT: If you want to pass the exam, you will have to study harder.

Single words, phrases, and subordinate clauses that begin a sentence are set off by a comma: *Yes, you may go. In my opinion, James Fenimore Cooper is unjustly ignored.* Sometimes short phrases do not require a comma.

*** comma with lists**

Disagreement exists as to whether or not a comma should be placed before the conjunctions *and*, *or*, or *nor* in a list.

I like cats, dogs, birds, and moles.
I like cats, dogs, birds and moles.

The first example illustrates the *serial comma*. Also called the *Oxford comma* and the *Harvard comma*, the serial comma is a comma placed before the conjunction.

Some usage guides recommend leaving out the last comma except in cases where confusion might arise because of another conjunction in the sentence. For example, the *Associated Press Stylebook* recommends:

The flag is red, white and blue. (no comma before "and")
BUT
I had orange juice, toast, and ham and eggs for breakfast. (comma before the "and" that introduces the third item which itself contains the word "and.")

Always using the serial comma eliminates the necessity of making decisions on a case by case basis. Choose a style guide that suits you and be consistent.

comma after main clause

INCORRECT: The King of Siam held absolute power over his subjects, when Anna Leonowens lived at his court.
CORRECT: The King of Siam held absolute power over his subjects when Anna Leonowens lived at his court.

When the adverbial clause follows the main clause, a comma is not usually needed.

comma or semi-colon?

INCORRECT: We missed the bus, we didn't know how to get home.
CORRECT: We missed the bus; we didn't know how to get home.

The **semi-colon** is used to join main clauses that

are not joined by a conjunction. However, if the clauses are very short, commas may be used: *He came, he saw, he conquered.*

Other uses of the semi-colon

- between clauses joined by words like *therefore, hence, however, nevertheless, accordingly, thus*, and *then*. For example, *We missed the train; therefore we were late for the concert.*

- between clauses even if there are conjunctions, if the clauses are long, or if the clauses contain commas. For example, *The new governor, I am told, is more honest than his predecessor; and he has already dismissed some of his staff, at least the most corrupt among them.*

- in lists when their inclusion prevents confusion. For example, *At the head table sat Charles Jetson, the team captain; Maryann Hill, the school secretary; Mario Lopez, the school principal; and Rusty Sample, the team mascot.*
- to introduce examples following the words *as, namely*, or *thus*. For example, *Three players were honored at the banquet; namely, Alex Baxter, Ferris Maxwell, and Percy Mitchell.*

Ellipsis

An **ellipsis** is the omission of one or more words in a sentence. The plural is **ellipses**.

The ellipsis has several uses, one of which is to shorten long quotations. The writer who condenses a statement needs to be sure that the edited version remains grammatically correct and true to the original thought that was expressed.

The **ellipsis mark** is a set of three dots [...]. The dots represent the missing word or words. Style guides differ as to whether the dots should be bracketed or not.

For rigorous academic or legal writing, writers are advised to consult a style book such as the *Chicago Manual of Style* or the *MLA Handbook*.

*** hyphen and dash**

Hyphens and dashes are short lines used in punctuation and spelling. Typographers work with dashes of different widths. The two most commonly used by the general writer are the **hyphen**, the **en dash**, and the **em dash**.

The **hyphen** is the narrowest of the three marks. The **en dash** is the width of the letter *n*; the **em dash** is the width of the letter *m*. Consult the directions for your word processing program to find out how to access the en and em dashes.

The hyphen is used to spell compound words: *dry-cleaning, long-anticipated, self-assured, ex-wife,* to divide words into syllables: *in-con-se-quen-tial,* and to separate numbers:*333-877-5555.*

The en dash is used with dates and page numbers:
The War Between the States (1861–1864)
The Conference will take place May 1–3
See pages 33-38.

The **em dash** is used to indicate a break in a sentence where a related thought is inserted: *I was running down the steps to the platform—as usual I was late—when I saw the man in the raincoat*. It can also be used to indicate an abrupt change in thought or attention: *Pass me the—what was that sound?*

The em dash is frequently used unnecessarily to replace more appropriate punctuation marks. For example,
My best friend—Colin Blakely—is acting at the Old Vic.

Here the name *Colin Blakely* is in apposition. If there is no reason for the added emphasis provided by dashes, commas are more appropriate:
My best friend, Colin Blakely, is acting at the Old Vic.

*NOTE: The *AP Style Book* directs writers to put a space on either side of the em dash. Most other style books do not.

multiple end marks

INCORRECT: We're going to Paris in April!!!! Do you want to go with us???

CORRECT: We're going to Paris in April! Do you want to go with us?

Multiple exclamation marks or question marks at the end of sentences are unnecessary and amateurish.

*** punctuation outside or inside the quotation mark**

American usage places the period inside the quotation marks whether the quoted material includes a period or not.

American usage:

She called him "an arrogant fool."

Polonius said, "Neither a borrower, nor a lender be."

British usage:

She called him "an arrogant fool".

Polonius said, "Neither a borrower, nor a lender be." (The period belongs to the quotation.)

quotation marks for emphasis

INCORRECT: All "anoraks" are now on sale.

CORRECT: All anoraks are now on sale.

The chief use of quotation marks is to set off the exact words used by a speaker or by another writer:

"You can't be serious," Percy said.
According to Dickens, the year 1775 was "the best of times" and "the worst of times."

An additional use of quotations marks is to indicate that the writer is using a word in an ironical sense: *Screaming at the top of her lungs, my "meek and mild" nanny sent the salesman running for his life.*

Using quotation marks merely for emphasis is unnecessary and confusing.

run-on sentence

INCORRECT: The fishing boat ran aground on a reef all the men were rescued.
CORRECT: The fishing boat ran aground on a reef. All the men were rescued.

A run-on sentence occurs when an independent clause follows another independent clause without punctuation or a joining word. The simplest way to correct such a sentence is to insert a period and capitalize the following word.

PART TWO

BASIC ENGLISH GRAMMAR

Maeve Maddox
and
Daniel Scocco

INTRODUCTION

Users of *100 Writing Mistakes to Avoid* who have forgotten some of their high school grammar can refresh their memory in the following pages.

Never fear, this review does not attempt to rehash every bit of English grammar found in a traditional school textbook. Its purpose is to present a brief review of only those grammar terms necessary to an understanding of the most common errors that occur in ordinary non-academic writing.

You don't have to know how to build an internal combustion engine in order to drive a car, but you do have to know such terms as *steering wheel, brake pedal*, and *hood release*.

It's not necessary to have a college degree in English in order to speak and write a standard form of your native language, but you do need to understand a few essential grammar terms.

Basic English Grammar is a review of the traditional English parts of speech and the parts of the sentence.

These definitions and examples were originally presented in electronic form to the readers of the popular language blog *DailyWritingTips.com/*. The blog's owner, Daniel Scocco, who owns the electronic rights, has kindly allowed this content to be reprinted here.

1. PARTS OF THE SENTENCE

The basic unit of speech and writing is the **sentence.**

A *sentence* is a group of words that forms a complete thought:

Birds fly.
Samuel Johnson's father ran a bookstore.
My two black cats enjoy lazing in the sun.

Every sentence is made up of two parts: the **subject**, which is what is being talked about, and the **predicate**, which is what is being said about the subject. The parts of the sentence may consist of a single word or several.

Subject	Predicate
Birds	fly
Samuel Johnson's father	ran a bookstore
My two black cats	enjoy lazing in the sun

1.1 SUBJECT

When we speak or write, we speak or write ABOUT something. The ***subject*** is what is being spoken about.

Birds fly. Birds are being talked about.
Samuel Johnson's father ran a bookstore. Samuel Johnson's father is being talked about.
My two black cats enjoy lazing in the sun. My two black cats are being talked about.

NOTE: The main word in the subject (usually a noun) is called the **simple subject.** The main word with all the words that describe it is called the **complete subject.** For example, in the second sentence above, the simple subject is "father." The complete subject is "Samuel Johnson's father."

1.2 PREDICATE

The predicate is what we say about the subject:

Birds fly. "fly" is what is being said about the birds; it's what they do.

Samuel Johnson's father ran a bookstore. "Ran" is what the father did; it's what is being said about him.

My two black cats enjoy lazing in the sun. "Enjoy" is what the cats do; it's what is being said about them.

NOTE: The main word in the predicate is a **verb**. The verb by itself is called the **simple predicate**. The verb plus any words or phrases that complete it or tell more about it make up the **complete predicate**. The simple predicate may contain more than one word because some tenses require helping verbs. For example, *The king has ruled the kingdom for seven years.* In this sentence, the simple predicate is "has ruled." The complete predicate is "has ruled the kingdom for seven years."

Action and State of Being

Most of the time the verb will denote an action, but not always. Sometimes a verb will denote a state of being or sensing. For example, *Toni Morrison is a celebrated author*. The verb "is" does not convey an action, but it is the main verb in this sentence.

Other verbs, such as *become* and *seem* do not describe an action, but a state of being. For example,
Edward VI became king at a young age.
You seem sad today.

COMMON ERROR: The predicate always contains a finite verb (one that indicates tense). A common writing fault is treating an nonfinite verb as if it were finite.

NOTE: A verb that shows time (present, past, future) is called a **finite verb.** A verb that does not indicate time is called a **nonfinite verb**.

INCORRECT: *All of us ~~laughing~~ in the water.*
CORRECT: *All of us **were laughing** in the water.*
OR *All of us **laughed** in the water.*

"Laughing" does not indicate present, past, or future time. The helping verbs *were* and the past form *laughed* with its *-ed* ending indicate time. Only a finite verb that shows present, past, or future time can be the main verb in a sentence.

NOTE: A sentence may be as short as one or two words, or much longer. For example,

Birds fly. (sentence)

Yesterday afternoon at about 5 p.m., large flocks of white birds were seen at an altitude of several hundred feet just off the coast of Scotland. (sentence)

When the first settlers arrived in North America, large flocks of birds called passenger pigeons often darkened the sky in flight, but, thanks to unregulated hunting, the passenger pigeon was reduced to extinction. (sentence)

OTHER PARTS OF THE SENTENCE

Additional information is added to the simple subject and predicate of a sentence with words or with word groups called **phrases** and **clauses**.

1.3 PHRASE

A phrase is a group of grammatically related words that does not contain a main verb. The words in the phrase act as a unit, usually functioning as a part of speech. For example,

The girl is ***at home*** *today, but tomorrow she is going* ***to the amusement park****.*

“At home” and “to the amusement park” are phrases functioning as adverbs of place.

Some teachers might refer to the words “The girl” as a phrase, but in this guide, only a group of words that does the work of a single part of speech is called a phrase.

1.4 CLAUSE

A clause is a group of grammatically related words that contains a main verb.

Some clauses can stand alone as complete sentences. Such clauses are called **main** or **independent clauses**.

For example,
The girl is at home today, but tomorrow she is going to the amusement park.
The two clauses in this sentence are of equal importance. The joining word "but" is simply a connecting word; it does not belong to either clause. Either clause, therefore, can stand alone, expressing a complete thought:

The girl is at home today. (complete thought; complete sentence)
Tomorrow she is going to the amusement park. (complete thought; complete sentence)

Other clauses are prevented from standing alone because they begin with words that limit their meaning, words like *because* and *when*. Such clauses are called **subordinate** or **dependent**

clauses. They depend upon another clause for their meaning.
For example,
The boy quit college because he won a talent show.

"The boy quit college" is a complete thought. It can stand alone as a complete sentence, so it is a main clause. "because he won a talent show" is an incomplete thought. The "because" leaves us wondering what went before, so the words cannot stand alone as a complete sentence. The clause is **subordinate** or **dependent**.

COMMON ERROR: A common writing fault is treating a subordinate or dependent clause as if it were a main clause:

> INCORRECT: When the battery ran down.
> CORRECT: When the battery ran down, we were left in the dark.

You'll find more more about clauses at Section 2.7.

1.5 OBJECT

An **object** is a word that receives the action of an action verb. For example,
The batter hit the ball.
The action of hitting has a receiver, “ball.” The ball receives the action and is therefore called the object of the verb.

There are two kinds: **direct object** and **indirect object**.

The word that receives the action of the verb is called its **direct object (DO).**

When the direct object passes to another receiver, the second receiver is the **indirect object (IO)**.

For example,
My mother writes me long letters.
The direct object is “letters,” the things that receive the action of writing.

The indirect object is “me,” the recipient of the direct object “letters.”
The indirect object usually comes directly after the verb.

To decide which is which, ask these questions about the verb:

1. Writes **what**? Answer, “letters.” *Letters* is the

direct object.
2. Writes **to whom** or **for whom**? Answer: "me."
Me is the indirect object

Some verbs that often take indirect objects are *write, send, tell, give, buy,* and *sell.*

1.6 COMPLEMENT

As noted above, not all verbs are action verbs. Only action verbs have objects. The other kinds of verb--being or sensing verbs--need a noun or adjective to complete their meaning. These words are called **complements** because they **complete** the meaning of the verb.

If the "completing" word is an adjective, it is called a **predicate adjective** (PA).

If the "completing" word is a noun or pronoun, it's called a **predicate noun** (PN).

*That actor is especially **handsome**.* (PA, completes the verb "is.")

*The young prince became **king**.* (PN, completes the verb "became.")

*Who is **this**?* (PN, completes the verb"is.")

2. THE PARTS OF SPEECH

Words are just words until they are used in a sentence. Once a word is used in a sentence, it becomes a **part of speech**. The function the word serves in a sentence is what makes it whatever part of speech it is.

For example, the word "run" can be used as more than one part of speech:
Sammy hit a home ***run****.* Here "run" is a noun functioning as the direct object of "hit."

You mustn't ***run*** *near the swimming pool.* Here "run" is a verb functioning as part of the main verb *must (not) run.*

The traditional eight parts of speech are: **noun, pronoun, adjective, verb, adverb, preposition, conjunction**, and **interjection**.

2.1 NOUN

A noun is a word used to describe a person, place, thing, event, idea, etc.

Nouns usually function as subjects or objects.

COMMON ERROR: The most important thing to remember about nouns is that they have "number." That means they can be singular or plural. A common writing error is to use a singular noun with a plural verb or a plural noun with a singular verb:

> INCORRECT: My favorite relatives ~~is~~ the ones who bring me presents.
> CORRECT: My favorite relatives **are** the ones who bring me presents.

NOUN CATEGORIES

Proper nouns

Used to describe a unique person or thing, proper nouns always start with a capital letter. Examples include *Mary, India*, and *Manchester United.*

Common nouns

Common nouns are used to describe persons or

things in general. Examples include *girl, country*, and *team.*

Concrete nouns

Nouns that can be perceived through the five senses are called concrete nouns. Examples include *ball, rainbow,* and *melody.*

Abstract nouns

Nouns that cannot be perceived through the five senses are called abstract nouns. Examples include *love, courage*, and *childhood.*

Countable nouns

Countable nouns can be counted. They have both singular and plural forms. Examples include *toys*, *children* and *books*.

Non-countable nouns

These nouns cannot (usually) be counted, and they don't have a plural form. Examples include *sympathy*, *laughter* and *oxygen*.

Forming the Plural of Nouns

The English language has regular and irregular plural forms of nouns.

The most common way to make a noun plural is to add -*s* to the singular: *car/cars*.

Certain terminal letter combinations follow

predictable rules:

- nouns ending with *-s, -x, -ch*, or *-sh*: add *-es*: *box/boxes; church/churches*
- nouns ending with a consonant followed by *-y*: change the *y* to *i* and add *-es*: *enemy/enemies*
- nouns ending in -o: add -es: *potato/potatoes*
  NOTE: many foreign borrowings, especially words from Italian, are exceptions to this rule: *canto/cantos, piano/pianos*
- nouns ending in *-is*: change *-is* to *-es* (e.g., *crisis/crises)*
- nouns ending in *-f*: change *-f* to *-v* and add *-es*: *wolf/wolves, calf/calves*
- nouns ending in *-fe*, change *-f* to *-v* and add *-s* *life/lives,* (pronounced with long *i*)

Some nouns form the plural by changing the internal vowels: *foot/feet, goose/geese, mouse/mice, louse/lice, man/men, woman/women, tooth/teeth*

Some nouns from the Latin form their plurals as they do in Latin, with *-i*, *-a*, or *ae*:
fungus/fungi, alumnus/alumni
phenomenon/phenomena, stratum/strata, datum/data,
alumna/alumnae, antenna/antennae

NOTE: Many of these Latin plurals have been anglicized so that one may also see the forms *funguses* and *antennas*. The plural noun *data* is commonly used as a singular. When in doubt, consult a dictionary or style guide.

Some nouns are spelled the same in the singular and in the plural: *one sheep/two sheep; one deer/two deer; one offspring/many offspring; one series/two series*

2.2 PRONOUN

The pronoun is used to replace nouns in order to avoid repetition. Compare:
Mary didn't go to school because Mary was sick.
Mary didn't go to school because she was sick.

In the second sentence, *she* is a personal pronoun used to replace "Mary." The word that a pronoun stands for is called its **antecedent**.

NOTE: Many of the most common grammatical errors arise from not understanding how to use pronouns.

Like nouns, pronouns have *number* (singular and plural).

Unlike nouns, pronouns also have special forms according to whether they are used as subjects or objects.

Personal Pronoun
Subject forms: *I, you, he, she, it, we, they*
Object forms: *me, you, him, her, it, us, them*

NOTE: In Modern English, second person has dwindled into one word, *you*. It's both singular and plural and can be used as either subject or object. Older English texts contain the archaic second person singular forms *thou* (subject) and *thee* (object) and the plural form *ye*.

COMMON ERROR: The most common error in the use of pronouns is to use an object form as a subject, or a subject form as an object:

> INCORRECT: ~~Me~~ and my friends like pizza.
> CORRECT: *My friends and **I** like pizza.*
>
> INCORRECT: They were very kind to Jack and ~~I~~.
> CORRECT: They were very kind to Jack and **me**.

Possessive Pronoun

mine, yours, his, hers, ours, theirs, its (The possessive pronoun for *thou* and *thee* is *thine.)*

NOTE: In this review I am careful to distinguish the **possessive adjectiv**es *(my, your, his, her, its, our,* and *their*) from the **possessive pronouns** (*mine, yours, his, hers, ours*, and *theirs*.) Many U.S. teachers do not make this distinction and call them all "pronouns." I prefer to make the distinction because the two types of word have different functions.

Unlike the *possessive adjective*, which comes before a noun and indicates possession, the *possessive pronoun* stands for a noun **and** indicates possession.

*This book is **mine**.* ("mine" stands for "book" and indicates that the book belongs to the speaker)

*This book is **yours**.* ("yours" stands for "book" and shows possession)

Here are two examples to illustrate the difference between a **possessive pronoun** and **possessive adjective**:
*This book is **mine**.* (possessive pronoun)
*This is **my** book.* (possessive adjective)

The possessive pronoun **stands in place** of a noun; the possessive adjective **describes** a noun.

Reflexive Pronoun
This special class of pronouns is used when the object is the same as the subject of the sentence: *myself, yourself, himself, herself, itself, ourselves, yourselves, themselves.*
For example, ***I** managed to cut **myself** while shaving*. (the action of the verb has an object that reflects the subject word)

COMMON ERROR: A common error in the use of the reflexive pronoun is to use it as a subject:

> INCORRECT: Jack and ~~myself~~ bought a house.
> CORRECT: Jack and **I** bought a house.

Another error with reflexive pronouns is the use of

nonstandard forms such as "hisself," "ourself," and "theirselves."

Interrogative Pronoun

what, which, who, whom, whose

These pronouns are used to introduce questions:
What are the odds?
Who left the door open?
Whom are you looking for? (Most U.S. speakers would probably say *"Who are you looking for?*)
Which is mine?

Demonstrative Pronoun

this, that, these, those.

These pronouns are used to stand for a noun and separate it from other things.
Is this the one you wanted?
Hand me those.
Generally speaking, use **this** and **these** to indicate items near the speaker and **that** and **those** for items farther away.

Notice that **demonstrative pronouns** replace nouns. The same words—*this, that, these,* and *those*—are also used as "demonstrative determiners" or **demonstrative adjectives**: *This house is ugly*. (Here "this" is pointing out the noun "house.")

Indefinite Pronoun

As the name implies, indefinite pronouns do not

refer to a specific thing, place or person. There are many of them, including *anyone, anywhere, everyone, none*, and *someone*.

Everyone is going to the party.
That's not anywhere I'd want to go.

Relative Pronoun

The relative pronouns are *that, who, whom, which, where, when*, and *why*. Like other pronouns the relative replaces a noun. Like conjunctions, relative pronouns function as joining words between clauses.

That's the man ***who*** *climbed Everest.* This"who" has more than one function. It stands for "man" and it links the main clause (*That's the man*) to the dependent clause (*who climbed Everest.*)
You'll find more about relative pronouns in Section 2.7.

2.3 ADJECTIVE

An adjective is a word that describes a noun. There are two main kinds: **attributive** and **predicative**.

An adjective is used *attributively* when it stands next to a noun and describes it.
*The **black** cat climbed a tree. (*attributive adjective*)*

An adjective is used predicatively when a verb separates it from the noun or pronoun it describes.
The umpire was **wrong**. (predicate adjective)
The crowd was **furious**. (predicate adjective)
She seems **tired** today. (predicate adjective)
This soup tastes **bad**. (predicate adjective)
The dog's coat feels **smooth**. (predicate adjective)

Verbs that can be completed by predicate adjectives are called **being verbs** or **copulative verbs**. They include all the forms of *to be,* and sensing verbs like *seem, feel,* and *taste*.

NOTE: certain verb forms may be also be used as adjectives:
*The man felt a **paralyzing** fear.* (present participle

verb form used to describe "fear")
Flavored *oatmeal tastes better than plain oatmeal.* (past participle verb form used to describe "oatmeal")

The usual place of the adjective in English is in front of the noun. You can have a whole string of adjectives if you like: *The* ***tall thin evil-looking*** *cowboy roped the* ***short fat inoffensive*** *calf.*

Sometimes, for rhetorical or poetic effect, the adjective can come after the noun:
Sarah ***Plain*** *and* ***Tall*** (book title)
This is the forest ***primeval.*** (poetic construction)

Adjective Classifications

- qualitative: *good, bad, happy, blue, French*
- possessive: *my, thy, his, her, its, our, your, their*
- relative and interrogative: *which, what, whatever,* etc.
- numeral: *one, two, second, single*, etc.
- indefinite: *some, any, much, few, every,* etc.
- demonstrative: *this, that, the, a (an), such*

NOTE: The demonstrative adjectives **the** and **a** (**an**) are so important in English that they have a special name: **articles**.

ARTICLES

The words **a**, **an**, and **the** are sometimes classed as a separate part of speech. In function, however, they can be grouped with the demonstrative adjectives that are used to point things out rather than describe them.

Definite Article
The is the definite article.

Indefinite Article
A is the indefinite article. **An** is the form of **a** used in front of a word that begins with a vowel sound.

The definite article is usually used to point out something that has already been introduced.

The indefinite article is used to introduce something unspecific, or something being introduced for the first time.

For example,
From the top of the rise we could see ***a*** *house. As we drew nearer, we could see that* ***the*** *house was a Victorian mansion.*

The article **a** derives from a word meaning "one." It is used with only singular nouns:
a katydid
an elephant

The can be used with either singular or plural nouns:

the boy/the boys

The indefinite article has two forms:
A is used before words beginning with a consonant sound or an aspirated h:
a car
a lamb
a hope
a habit
a hotel

An is used before words beginning with a vowel sound:
an ape
an image
an untruth
an honorable man

The plural of **a/an** is **some**.
*I want **a** toy.* (singular)
*I want **some** toys.* (plural)

2.4 VERB

The verb is the heart of the sentence. Verb errors can be avoided if one understands the following terms:
principal parts, person, number, transitive, intransitive, tense, voice, and *mood.*

Principal parts of the Verb

The writer who knows the three principal parts of the verb is able to build any tense.

The three principal parts of the verb are: **present, past**, and **past participle**.

The *past participle* form of the verb is the form used with *has* or *have*. For example, the principal parts of the regular verb *to walk* are *walk,walked*,(have)*walked.* The principal parts of the irregular verb *to do* are *do, did, (have) done.*

Regular verbs

Most English verbs are **regular**. That means that they form the simple past and the past participle by adding the **-ed** ending.

Irregular verbs

Irregular verbs form the past by changes in

spelling. For that reason the principal parts of the irregular verbs must be memorized.

The most common error that occurs with the use of irregular verbs is to use the simple past form where the past participle form is called for. For example, *Jack has went to the store* instead of *Jack has gone to the store.*

The most effective way to learn the irregular verb forms is to recite the principal parts of each verb numerous times, always including the word *has* or *have* in front of the past participle form. For example,

go, went, (has) *gone*
sing, sang, (has) *sung*
do, did, (has) *done*

Person
Verbs are said to have "person."

First person is the form of the verb used with the subject pronouns *I* and *we*.

Second person is the form of the verb used with the subject pronoun *you.*

Third person is the form of the verb used with the subject pronouns *he, she, it,* and *they.*

Number
Verbs are are either *singular* or *plural* in number. Compare the following sentences,

The king believes in justice.
(The singular subject "king" takes a singular verb, "believes.")

The people believe in justice.
(The plural subject "people" takes a plural verb, "believe.")

The only time that singular and plural English verbs differ in spelling is in the present tense. For example, here are the present tense forms of the regular verb **to walk**:

1st person singular, *I walk*
2nd person singular, *you walk*
3rd person singular, *he/she/it walks*
1st person plural, *we walk*
2nd person plural, *you walk*
3rd person plural, *they walk*

Note that only the 3rd person singular differs by adding an *s*.

More examples of singular and plural subjects and verbs:
Sallie sings. (singular subject, singular verb)
We sing with her. (plural subject, plural verb)

My dog seldom barks. (singular subject, singular verb)
The dogs next door bark all night long. (plural subject, plural verb)

Kinds of Verb

English has three kinds of verbs: *transitive, intransitive*, and *incomplete*.

1. Transitive Verbs

A verb is transitive when the action is carried across to a receiver:
The farmer grows potatoes.
Elvis sang ballads.

The receiver of an action is called its **direct object (DO)**. The DO answers the question "What?" or "Whom? after the verb. Grows what? Potatoes. Sang what? Ballads.

2. Intransitive Verbs

A verb is intransitive when the action stays with the verb. It is not carried across to a receiver:
Corn grows.
Elvis sang.
NOTE: Adding a prepositional phrase to modify the verb does not change the fact that the action of the verb remains with the subject: For example,

Corn grows in the fields.
Elvis sang all over the world.

The phrases "in the fields" and "all over the world" simply add information about the verbs.

Both transitive and intransitive verbs are action verbs.

3. Incomplete Verbs
There are three types of incomplete verbs:
i. being verbs - also called linking or copulative verbs:
to be, seem, become, taste, smell, sound, feel

Tip: Some of these verbs can also be used transitively. If in doubt, substitute a form of *to be* for the verb. If the sentence still makes sense, the verb is being used as a linking verb. For example: *He **feels** depressed. He **is** depressed.* The replacement makes sense. "Feels" is a linking verb.

*He **feels** the wall. He **is** the wall.* The replacement is nonsense. "Feels" is not a linking verb. It's a transitive action verb.

ii. auxiliary verbs - also called "helping verbs": *be, have, shall, will, do,* and *may*.

iii. semi-auxiliary verbs
must, can, ought, dare, need.

These auxiliary verbs are used to form different

tenses, voices, and moods. Some of them, like *have* and *do*, can be used as complete verbs. Most of them, like *shall* and *may*, do not exist as complete verbs. For example, one can **do** something, but one cannot **may** something.

Voice

English verbs are said to have two voices: **active** and **passive**.

Active Voice: the subject of the sentence performs the action:

His son catches fly balls.
Creative children often dream in class.

NOTE: Verbs in the active voice may be either transitive or intransitive.

Passive Voice: the subject receives the action:
The ball was caught by the first baseman.
The duty is performed by the new recruits.
The dough was beaten by the mixer.
The mailman was bitten by the dog.

NOTE: Only transitive verbs can be used in the passive voice. What would be the direct object of the verb in the active voice becomes the subject of the verb in the passive voice:

Active voice: *The dog bit the mailman.* "bit" is a

transitive verb. The receiver/direct object is "mailman."

Passive voice: *The mailman was bitten by the dog.* "bit" is now in the passive voice. The "receiver" has become the subject of the verb.

A passive verb in either present or past tense will always have two parts: some form of the verb *to be (am, is, are, was, were)*, and a past participle (verb form ending in **-ed, -en**, or any form used with **have** when forming a perfect tense).

NOTE: The mere presence of the verb *to be* does not indicate that a verb is in the passive voice. The test of a verb in the passive voice is this question: "Is the subject performing the action of the verb, or is the subject receiving the action of the verb?" If the subject is receiving the action, then the verb is in passive voice. Sometimes the passive voice is the best way to express a thought. Used carelessly, however, passive voice can produce a ponderous, inexact writing style.

Mood

English verbs have four moods: *indicative, imperative, subjunctive*, and *infinitive*.

Mood is the form of the verb that shows the mode or manner in which a thought is expressed.

Indicative Mood: expresses an assertion, denial, or question:
Little Rock is the capital of Arkansas.
Ostriches cannot fly.
Have you finished your homework?

Imperative Mood: expresses command, prohibition, entreaty, or advice:
Don't smoke in this building.
Be careful!
Don't drown that puppy!

Subjunctive Mood: expresses doubt or something contrary to fact.

Modern English speakers use indicative mood most of the time, resorting to a kind of "mixed subjunctive" that makes use of helping verbs: *If I should see him, I will tell him.*
American speakers are more likely to say:
If I see him, I will tell him.

The verb *may* can be used to express a wish:
May you have many more birthdays.
May you live long and prosper.

The verb *were* can also indicate the use of the subjunctive:
If I were you, I wouldn't keep driving on those tires.
If he were governor, we'd be in better fiscal shape.

The use of *were* in sentences like this is losing ground. Many speakers use *was* instead.

Infinitive Mood: expresses an action or state without reference to any subject. It does not indicate time. It can be the source of sentence fragments when the writer mistakenly thinks the infinitive form is a fully functioning verb.

When we speak of the "infinitive," we usually mean the basic form of the verb with "to" in front of it:
to go
to sing
to walk
Verbs in the "infinitive mood" include participle forms ending in **-ed** and **-ing**. Verbs in the infinitive mood are not being used as verbs, but as other parts of speech.

To err is human; to forgive, divine.
"to err" and "to forgive" are infinitives being used as nouns.

He is a man to be admired.
"to be admired" is an infinitive phrase used as an adjective, the equivalent of "admirable" It describes the noun "man."

He came to see you.

"to see you" is an infinitive phrase used as an adverb to tell why he came.

Tense

Modern English has six tenses, each of which has a corresponding continuous tense.

The first three tenses, *present, pas*t, and *future*, present few problems:

He lives in Canada. They live in the United States. (present) NOTE: The present singular differs from the other present verbs by adding **s**.
I lived in England for seven years. (simple past)
Charles will live with his father next year. (future)

The other three tenses, *perfect*, *past perfect (*also called the *pluperfect)*, and *future perfect*, are formed with the helping verbs *have, has*, and *had*.

perfect: used to express an event that has finished and to describe an event which, although in the past, has effects that continue into the present:
Queen Elizabeth has reigned for 60 years.

past perfect (pluperfect): used to express an event that took place before another action also in the past:
I had driven all the way to Oklahoma when I realized my mistake.

future perfect: used to express an event that will have taken place at some time in the future: *As of February 26, I shall have been in this job for six years.*

NOTE:
The continuous tenses are formed by adding the appropriate helping verbs to an *-ing* verb. For example,
I am driving. (present continuous)
I will be driving. (future continuous)

2.5 ADVERB

Adverbs are used to describe or modify a verb, adjective, clause, or another adverb. Basically, they modify everything except nouns and pronouns. ("Modify" means to add to or limit the meaning of a word.)

Adverb modifying a verb:
*He was running **fast**.* ("fast" modifies "running")

Adverb modifying an adjective:
*She took a **very** small piece of the cake*. ("very" modifies "small")

Adverb modifying a sentence:
Strangely, *the man left the room.* ("strangely" modifies the whole sentence)

Adverbs answer the following questions:
"When?" (adverbs of time)
"Where?" (adverbs of place)
"How?" (adverbs of manner)

Conjunctive Adverbs
These adverbs act rather like conjunctions. Not true

conjunctions, they require the addition of a semi-colon after the clause that precedes them:
You broke the law; therefore you must go to prison.
Words used as conjunctive adverbs:

accordingly	meanwhile
also	moreover
anyway	namely
again	nevertheless
besides	next
certainly	nonetheless
consequently	now
contrarily	otherwise
finally	rather
further	similarly
furthermore	so
elsewhere	subsequently
hence	still
henceforth	that is
however	then
in contrast	thereafter
incidentally	therefore
indeed	thus
instead	undoubtedly
likewise	

2.6 PREPOSITION

Prepositions are used to link nouns and pronouns to other words within a sentence. A group of words that begins with a preposition and ends with a noun or pronoun is called a **prepositional phrase**. The word that ends the phrase is called the **object of the preposition**.

Usually prepositions show a spatial or temporal relationship between the noun and the object:
The cat is under the table.
"Cat" is the noun. "Under" is the preposition. "Table" is the object of the preposition.

Words commonly used as prepositions:

about above after among around along at	before, behind beneath beside between by down	from in into like near of off	on out over through to up upon under with

NOTE: prepositional phrases do the work of adverbs and adjectives:

Adverbial phrase
The dog was hiding under the porch.
The prepositional phrase “under the porch” acts as an adverb, specifying where the dog was hiding.

Adjectival phrase
The dog in the wagon barked incessantly.
The prepositional phrase “in the wagon” acts as an adjective, specifying which dog is barking.

2.7 CONJUNCTION

A conjunction joins words and groups of words.

The two classes of conjunction are **coordinate** (or coordinating) and **subordinate** (or subordinating).

Coordinate conjunctions

one-word coordinating conjunctions:

and
but
for
or
nor
so
yet

Correlative conjunctions (word pairs):

either…or
neither…nor

Mother and Father are driving me to New Orleans. (*and* is a coordinate conjunction joining words of equal significance in the sentence.)

I painted the walls, but Jack painted the woodwork. (*but* is a coordinate conjunction joining clauses of equal significance in the sentence. Either clause could stand alone as a sentence.)

Subordinate conjunctions:
that
as
after
before
since
when
where
unless
if

Because you can't get away, we'll go without you. *Because* is a subordinate conjunction joining a less important thought to a more important thought. The main clause, "we'll go without you," can stand alone as a complete thought. The subordinate clause, "Because you can't get away," is an incomplete thought. It is dependent upon the main clause for meaning.

NOTE: The relative pronouns *that, who, whom, which, where, when*, and *why* are used in the same way that subordinate conjunctions are. The difference is that the relative pronouns serve three purposes at once:

1. They stand for a noun in the main clause
2. They connect clauses

3. They serve as a subject or object word in the subordinate clause.

• *He is the man who invented the hula hoop.* ("who" stands for "man" and is the subject of "invented")
• *Charles is the boy whom the other children tease.* ("whom" stands for "boy" and is the object of "tease")
• *Give me the piece of string that is waxed.* ("that" stands for "string" and is the subject of "is waxed")
• *That horse, which won the Derby last year, is for sale.* ("which" refers to "horse" and is the subject of "won"

The possessive adjective *whose* can also be used to join clauses:
That's the bird whose plumage I admire. ("whose" refers to "bird" and describes "plumage"

2.8 INTERJECTION

The word *interjection* comes from from a Latin word that means "throw between." An interjection is a word or phrase that is thrown into a sentence to express an emotion:

***Goodness**, how you've grown!*
***Darn**, I forgot my lunch!*
***Alas**, will he never return?*

All the impolite expressions that we call "expletives" are interjections.

Strictly speaking, an interjection is not a part of speech. It serves no grammatical function but is rather, according to grammarian F. J. Rahtz, "a noisy utterance like the cry of an animal."

Use them judiciously.

CONCLUSION

It's probably safe to say that no one speaks standard English all of the time. Language is a personal matter and we choose our words as we choose our clothing: different items for different occasions.

In one sense, there is no "right way" or "wrong way" to speak English. Every regional dialect is a complete and valid mode of expression in its local context. What we call "standard English" is itself a dialect. Because English is spoken by so many people of different origins, the ability to speak and write a standard dialect in addition to one's home dialect is a useful social skill and a valuable business asset.

It's hoped that the material in this book will enable you to avoid the most common errors of Standard English that can interfere with the message you wish to convey.

ABOUT THE AUTHOR

Maeve Maddox is a freelance writer who holds a B.A. (Honours) in English from the University of London and a Ph.D. in Comparative Literature from the University of Arkansas at Fayetteville. She has taught English at every level from pre-school to university.

Her academic credentials are in the name Margaret Joan Maddox.

Her academic writing includes *Portrayals of Joan of Arc in Film* and the representative essay on Joan of Arc in the textbook *Icons of the Middle Ages*.

Email: drmaddox@mac.com
Author's website: maevemaddox.com
Teaching website: americanenglishdoctor.com

PUBLICATIONS

As Maeve Maddox

100 Writing Mistakes to Avoid
A bare-bones style guide for writers in a hurry.
ISBN: 978-1470137861 (print)
Kindle edition ASIN: B00B5J5BQI

A Joan for All Seasons: Joan of Arc in History and the Movies. A film guide to six Joan of Arc movies.
ISBN: 978-0984786114 (print)
ISBN: 978-0986786121 (digital)

So You Want to Write!
Fifty essays on the writing craft.
ISBN: 978-0984786107 (print)

As Margaret Joan Maddox

Portrayals of Joan of Arc in Film: From the Historical Joan to Her Mythological Daughters.
ISBN: 978-0773449459

"Joan of Arc." pages 417-449. *Icons of the Middle Ages: Rulers, Rebels, and Saints*. Volume 2. Edited by Lister M. Matheson.
ISBN: 978-0-313-34080-2

As Peggy Maddox

"Ravishing Marie: Eugene Mason's Translation of Marie de France's Breton Lai of Lanval," *Translation Review*, No. 63, 2002.

"Retiring the Maid: The Last Joan of Arc Movie," *Journal of Religion and Popular Culture*, Volume III. Spring 2003.

Made in the USA
Middletown, DE
01 July 2020